C000170926

MEMOIRS

of a

MONTICELLO SLAVE

As Dictated to Charles Campbell
in the 1840's by Isaac, one of
Thomas Jefferson's Slaves

UNIVERSITY OF VIRGINIA PRESS
CHARLOTTESVILLE. VIRGINIA

FOREWORD

The reminiscences printed here were
taken down in the 1840's by Charles Campbell, the Virginia historian, from the verbal
account of a slave who had lived at Monticello from 1775 until two years before Jefferson's death. They were first printed in
1951 in a scholarly edition with introduction and notes by Dr. Rayford W. Logan,
which was sold out within a year of its first
issue.

The present popular edition is intended
to meet the growing demand for this classic.

TABLE OF CONTENTS

ILLUSTRATIONS

For acknowledgments and details concerning the illustrations, see pages 69-72.

CHAPTER 1

ISAAC JEFFERSON was born at Monticello: his mother was named Usler[1] but nicknamed Queen, because her husband was named George and commonly called King George. She was pastry-cook and washerwoman: stayed in the laundry. Isaac toated wood for her: made fire and so on. Mrs. Jefferson would come out there with a cookery book in her hand and read out of it to Isaac's mother how to make cakes, tarts and so on.

Mrs. Jefferson was named Patsy Wayles,[2] but when Mr. Jefferson married her she was the widow Skelton, widow of Batter[3] Skelton. Isaac was one year's child with Patsy Jefferson: she was suckled part of the time by

Isaac's mother. Patsy married Thomas Mann Randolph.[4] Mr. Jefferson bought Isaac's mother from Col. William Fleming of Goochland. Isaac remembers John Nelson, an Englishman at work at Monticello: he was an inside worker, a finisher. The blacksmith was Billy Ore;[5] the carriage-maker Davy Watson: he worked also for Colonel Carter of Blenheim, eight miles from Monticello. Monticello-house was pulled down in part and built up again some six or seven times. One time it was struck by lightning. It had a Franklin rod at one end. Old Master used to say, "If it hadn't been for that Franklin the whole house would have gone." They was forty years at work upon that house before Mr. Jefferson stopped building.

CHAPTER 2

MR. JEFFERSON came down to Williamsburg in a phaeton made by Davy Watson. Billy Ore did the iron-work.[6] That phaeton was sent to London and the springs &c was gilded. This was when Mr. Jefferson was in Paris. Isaac remembers coming down to Williamsburg in a wagon at the time Mr. Jefferson was Governor. He came down in the phaeton: his family with him in a coach and four. Bob Hemings drove the phaeton; Jim Hemings was a body-servant; Martin Hemings the butler. These three were brothers[7]: Mary Hemings and Sally, their Sisters. Jim and Bob bright mulattoes; Martin, darker. Jim and Martin rode on horseback. Bob went afterwards to live with old Dr. Strauss in Richmond and unfortunately had his hand shot off with a blunderbuss. Mary Hemings rode in the wagon. Sally Hemings' mother Betty was a bright mulatto woman, and Sally mighty near white: she was the youngest child. Folks said that these Hemingses was old Mr. Wayles' children. Sally was very handsome: long straight hair down her back. She was about eleven years old when Mr. Jefferson took her to France to wait on Miss Polly. She and Sally went out to France a year after Mr. Jefferson went. Patsy went with him at first, but she carried no maid with her. Harriet, one of Sally's daughters, was very handsome. Sally had a son named Madison, who learned to be a great fiddler. He has been in Petersburg twice: was here when the balloon went up—the balloon that Beverly sent off.

Mr. Jefferson drove faster in the phaeton than the wagon. When the wagon reached Williamsburg Mr. Jefferson was living in the College.[8] Isaac and the rest of the servants stayed in the Assembly-house—a long wooden building. Lord Botetourt's picture[9] was there. The Assembly-house had a gallery on top running round to the College. There was a well there then: none there now. Some white people was living in one end of the house: a man named Douglas was there: they called him Parson Douglas.[10] Mr. Jefferson's room in the College was down stairs. A tailor named Giovanni, an Italian, lived there too: made clothes for Mr. Jefferson and his servants. Mrs. Jefferson was there with Patsy and Polly.[11] Mrs. Jefferson was small: she drawed from old Madam Byrd[12] several hundred people and then married a rich man.[13] Old Master had twelve quarters seated with black people: but mighty few come by him: he want rich himself—only his larnin. Patsy Jefferson was tall like her father; Polly low like her mother and long-ways the handsomest: pretty lady jist like her mother: pity she died—poor thing! She married John W. Eppes—a handsome man, but had a hare-lip.

Jupiter and John drove Mr. Jefferson's coach and four: one of em rode postilion: they rode postilion in them days. Travelling in the phaeton Mr. Jefferson used oftentimes to take the reins himself and drive. Whenever he wanted to travel fast *he'd* drive:

would drive powerful hard himself. Jupiter and John wore caps and gilded bands. The names of the horses was Senegore, Gustavus, Otter, Remus, Romulus, and Caractacus, Mr. Jefferson's riding-horse.

CHAPTER 3

AFTER one year the Government was moved from Williamsburg to Richmond. Mr. Jefferson moved there with his servants, among em Isaac. It was cold weather when they moved up. Mr. Jefferson lived in a wooden house near where the Palace[14] stands now. Richmond was a small place then: not more than two brick houses in the town: all wooden houses what there was. At that time from where the Powhatan house now stands clear down to the Old Market was pretty much in pines. It was a wooden house shedded round like a barn on the hill, where the Assembly-men used to meet, near where the Capitol stands now. Old Mr. Wiley had a saddler-shop in the same house. Isaac knew Billy Wiley mighty well—a saddler by trade: he was door-keeper at the Assembly. His wife was a baker and baked bread and ginger-cakes. Isaac would go into the bake-oven and make fire for. She had a great big bake oven. Isaac used to go way into the oven: when he came out Billy Wiley would chuck wood in. She some-times gave Isaac a loaf of bread or a cake. One time she went up to Monticello to see Mr. Jefferson. She saw Isaac there and gave him a ninepence and said, "This is the boy that made fires for me." Mr. Jefferson's family-servants then at the palace were Bob Hemings, Martin, Jim, house-servants; Jupi-ter and John, drivers; Mary Hemings and young Betty Hemings, seamstress and house-woman; Sukey, Jupiter's wife, the cook.

CHAPTER 4

THE day before the British[15] came to Richmond Mr. Jefferson sent off his family in the carriage. Bob Hemings and Jim drove. When the British was expected[16] Old Master kept the spy-glass and git up by the sky-light window to the top of the palace looking towards Williamsburg. Some other gentlemen went up with him, one of them old Mr. Marsdell: he owned where the basin is now and the basin-spring. Isaac used to fetch water from there up to the palace. The British reached Manchester about 1 o'clock.[17] Isaac larnt to beat drum about this time. Bob Anderson, a white man, was a blacksmith. Mat Anderson was a black man and worked with Bob. Bob was a fifer, Mat was a drummer. Mat bout that time was sort a-makin love to Mary Hemings. The soldiers at Richmond, in the camp at Bacon Quarter Branch, would come every two or three days to salute the Governor at the Palace, marching about there drumming and fifing. Bob Anderson would go into the house to drink; Mat went into the kitchen to see Mary Hemings. He would take his drum with him into the kitchen and set it down there. Isaac would beat on it and Mat larnt him how to beat.

CHAPTER 5

AS soon as the British formed a line, three cannon was wheeled round all at once and fired three rounds. Till they fired, the Richmond people thought they was a company come from Petersburg to join them: some of em even hurraed when they see them coming: but that moment they fired every body knew it was the British. One of the cannon-balls knocked off the top of a butcher's house: he was named Daly, not far from the Governor's house. The butcher's wife screamed out and hollerd and her children too and all. In ten minutes not a white man was to be seen in Richmond: they ran as hard as they could stave to the camp at Bacon Quarter Branch.

There was a monstrous hollering and screaming of women and children. Isaac was out in the yard: his mother ran out and cotch him up by the hand and carried him into the kitchen hollering. Mary Hemings, she jerked up her daughter the same way. Isaac run out again in a minute and his mother too: she was so skeered, she didn't know whether to stay indoors or out. The British was dressed in red. Isaac saw them marching. The horsemen (Simcoe's cavalry) was with them: they come arter the artillery-men. They formed in line and marched up to the Palace with drums beating: it was an awful sight: seemed like the day of judgment was come. When they fired the cannon Old Master called out to John to fetch his horse Caractacus from the stable and rode off.

CHAPTER 6

ISAAC never see his Old Master arter dat for six months. When the British come in, an officer rode up and asked "Whar is the Governor?" Isaac's father (George) told him, "He's gone to the mountains." The officer said, "Whar is the keys of the house?" Isaac's father gave him the keys: Mr. Jefferson had left them with him. The officer said, "Whar is the silver?" Isaac's father told him, "It was all sent up to the mountains." The old man had put all the silver about the house in a bed-tick and hid it under a bed in the kitchen and saved it too and got his freedom by it. But he continued to sarve Mr. Jefferson and had forty pounds from Old Master and his wife. Isaac's mother had seven dollars a month for lifetime for washing, ironing, and making pastry. The British sarcht the house but didn't disturb none of the furniture: but they plundered the wine-cellar, rolled the pipes out and stove em in, knockin the heads out. The bottles they broke the necks off with their swords, drank some, threw the balance away. The wine-cellar was full: Old Master had plenty of wine and rum—the best: used to have Antigua rum, twelve years old. The British next went to the corn-crib and took all the corn out, strewed it in a line along the street towards where the Washington tavern[18] is now (1847) and brought their horses and fed them on it: took the bridles off. The British said they didn't want anybody but the Governor: didn't want to hurt him; only wanted to put a pair of silver handcuffs on him: had brought them along with them on purpose. While they was plunderin they took all of the meat out of the meat-house; cut it up, laid it out in parcels: every man took his ration and put it in his knapsack. When Isaac's mother found they was gwine to car him away she thought they was gwine to leave her. She was cryin and hollerin when one of the officers came on a horse and ordered us all to Hylton's. Then they marched off to Westham. Isaac heard the powder-magazine when it blew up—like an earthquake. Next morning between eight and nine they marched to Tuckahoe, fifteen miles: took a good many colored people from Old Tom Mann Randolph. He was called "Tuckahoe Tom." Isaac has often been to Tuckahoe—a low-built house but monstrous large. From Tuckahoe the British went to Daniel Hylton's. They carred off thirty people from Tuckahoe and some from Hylton's. When they come back to Richmond they took all Old Master's from his house: all of em had to walk except Daniel and Molly (children of Mary the pastry-cook) and Isaac. He was then big enough to beat the drum: but couldn't raise it off the ground: would hold it tilted over to one side and beat on it that way.

CHAPTER 7

THERE was about a dozen wagons along: they (the British) pressed the common wagons: four horses to a wagon: some black drivers, some white: every wagon guarded by ten men marching alongside.

One of the officers give Isaac name Sambo: all the time feedin him: put a cocked hat on his head and a red coat on him and all laughed. Coat a monstrous great big thing: when Isaac was in it couldn't see nothin of it but the sleeves dangling down. He remembers crossing the river somewhere in a periauger [piragua]. And so the British carred them all down to Little York (Yorktown.) They marched straight through town and camped jist below back of the battle-field. Mr. Jefferson's people there was Jupiter, Sukey the cook, Usley (Isaac's mother), George (Isaac's father), Mary the seamstress, and children Molly, Daniel, Joe, Wormley, and Isaac. The British treated them mighty well, give em plenty of fresh meat and wheat bread. It was very sickly at York: great many colored people died there, but none of Mr. Jefferson's folks. Wallis (Cornwallis) had a cave dug and was hid in there. There was tremendous firing and smoke: seemed like heaven and earth was come together: every time the great guns fire Isaac jump up off the ground. Heard the wounded men hollerin. When the smoke blow off you see the dead men laying on the ground. General Washington brought all Mr. Jefferson's folks and about twenty of Tuckahoe Tom's (Tom Mann Randolph's) back to Richmond with him and sent word to Mr. Jefferson to send down to Richmond for his servants. Old Master sent down two wagons right away and all of em that was carred away went up back to Monticello. At that time Old Master and his family was at Poplar Forest, his place in Bedford. He stayed there after his arm was broke, when Caractacus threw him. Old Master was mightly pleased to see his people come back safe and sound[19] and to hear of the plate.

CHAPTER 8

MR. JEFFERSON was a tall strait-bodied man as ever you see, right square-shouldered: nary man in this town walked so straight as my Old Master: neat a built man as ever was seen in Vaginny, I reckon, or any place—a straight-up man[20]: long face, high nose.

Jefferson Randolph (Mr. Jefferson's grandson) nothing like him, except in height—tall, like him: not built like him: Old Master was a straight-up man. Jefferson Randolph pretty much like his mother. Old Master wore Vaginny cloth and a red waistcoat, (all the gentlemen wore red waistcoats in dem days) and small clothes: arter dat he used to wear red breeches too.[21] Governor

Page used to come up there to Monticello, wife and daughter wid him: drove four-in hand: servants John, Molly and a postilion. Patrick Henry visited Old Master: coach and two: his face for all the world like the images of Bonaparte: would stay a week or more. Mann Page used to be at Monticello— a plain mild-looking man: his wife and daughter along with him. Dr. Thomas Walker lived about ten miles from Monti-cello—a thin-faced man. John Walker[22] (of Belvoir), his brother, owned a great many black people.

CHAPTER 9

OLD Master was never seen to come out before breakfast—about 8 o'clock. If it was warm weather he wouldn't ride out till evening: studied upstairs till bell ring for dinner. When writing he had a copyin machine: while he was a-writin he wouldn't suffer nobody to come in his room: had a dumb-waiter: when he wanted anything he had nothin to do but turn a crank and the dumb-waiter would bring him water or fruit on a plate or anything he wanted. Old Master had abundance of books: sometimes would have twenty of 'em down on the floor at once: read fust one, then tother. Isaac has often wondered how Old Master came to have such a mighty head: read so many of them books: and when they go to him to ax him anything, he go right straight to the book and tell you all about it. He talked French and Italian. Madzay[23] talked with him: his place was called Colle. General Redhazel (Riedesel) stayed there. He (Mazzei) lived at Monticello with Old Master some time: Didiot, a Frenchman, married his daughter Peggy: a heavy chunky looking woman—mighty handsome. She had a daughter Frances and a son Francis: called the daughter Franky. Mazzei brought to Monticello Antonine, Jovanini, Francis, Modena, and Belligrini, all gardiners. My Old Master's garden was monstrous large: two rows of palings, all round ten feet high.

CHAPTER 10

MR. JEFFERSON had a clock in his kitchen at Monticello; never went into the kitchen except to wind up the clock. He never would have less than eight covers at dinner—if nobody at table but himself: had from eight to thirty two covers for dinner: plenty of wine, best old Antigua rum and cider: very fond of wine and water. Isaac never heard of his being disguised in drink. He kept three fiddles: played in the arternoons and sometimes arter supper. This was in his early time. When he begin to git so old, he didn't play: kept a spinnet made mostly in shape of a harpsichord: his daughter played on it. Mr. Fauble, a Frenchman that lived at Mr.

Walker's, a music-man, used to come to Monticello and tune it. There was a forte piano and a guitar there: never seed anybody play on them but the French people. Isaac never could git acquainted with them: could hardly larn their names. Mr. Jefferson always singing when ridin or walkin: hardly see him anywhar out doors but what he was a-singin:[24] had a fine clear voice, sung minnits (minuets) and sich: fiddled in the parlor. Old Master very kind to servants.

CHAPTER 11

THE fust year Mr. Jefferson was elected President,[25] he took Isaac on to Philadelphia: he was then about fifteen years old: travelled on horseback in company with a Frenchman named Joseph Rattiff and Jim Hemings, a body-servant. Fust day's journey they went from Monticello to old Nat Gordon's, on the Fredericksburg road, next day to Fredericksburg, then to Georgetown, crossed the Potomac there, and so to Philadelphia: eight days a-goin. Had two ponies and Mr. Jefferson's tother riding-horse Odin. Mr. Jefferson went in the phaeton: Bob Hemings drove: changed horses on the road. When they got to Philadelphia, Isaac stayed three days at Mr.

Jefferson's house: then he was bound prentice to one Bringhouse, a tinner: he lived in the direction of the Water-works. Isaac remembers seeing the image of a woman thar holding a goose in her hand—the water spouting out of the goose's mouth. This was at the head of Market Street. Bringhouse was a short, mighty small, neat-made man: treated Isaac very well: went thar to larn the tinner's trade: fust week larnt to cut out and sodder: make little pepper-boxes and graters and sich, out of scraps of tin, so as not to waste any till he had larnt. Then to making cups. Every Sunday Isaac would go to the President's House—large brick house, many windows: same house Ginral Washington lived in before when he was President. Old Master used to talk to me mighty free and ax me, "how you come on Isaac, larnin de tin-business?" As soon as he could make cups pretty well he carred three or four to show him. Isaac made four dozen pint-cups a day and larnt to tin copper and sheets (sheet-iron)—make 'em tin. He lived four years with Old Bringhouse. One time Mr. Jefferson sent to Bringhouse to tin his copper-kittles and pans for kitchen use: Bringhouse sent Isaac and another prentice thar—a white boy named Charles: can't think of his other name. Isaac was the only black boy in Bringhouse's shop. When Isaac carred the cups to his Old Master to show him, he was mightily pleased: said, "Isaac you are larnin mighty fast: I bleeve I must send you back to Vaginny to car on the tin-business. You is growin too big: no use for you to stay here no longer."

Arter dat Mr. Jefferson sent Isaac back to Monticello to car on the tin-business thar. Old Master bought a sight of tin for the purpose. Mr. Jefferson had none of his family with him in Philadelphia. Polly his daughter stayed with her Aunt Patsy Carr: she lived seven or eight miles from Old Master's great house. Sam Carr was Mr. Jefferson's sister's child. There were three brothers of the Carrs—Sam, Peter and Dabney. Patsy Jefferson, while her father was President in Philadelphia, stayed with Mrs. Eppes at Wintopoke: Mrs. Eppes was a sister of Mrs. Jefferson—mightily like her sister. Frank Eppes was a big heavy man.

Old Master's servants at Philadelphia was Bob and Jim Hemings; Joseph Rattiff, a

Frenchman, the hostler. Mr. Jefferson used to ride out on horseback in Philadelphia. Isaac went back to Monticello. When the tin came they fixed up a shop. Jim Bringhouse came on to Monticello all the way with Old Master to fix up the shop and start Isaac to work: Jim Bringhouse stayed thar more than a month.

CHAPTER 12

ISAAC knew old Colonel (Archibald) Cary mighty well: as dry a looking man as ever you see in your life. He has given Isaac more whippings than he has fingers and toes. Mr. Jefferson used to set Isaac to open gates for Colonel Cary: there was three gates to open, the furst bout a mile from the house:tother one three quarters; then the yard-gate, at the stable three hundred yards from the house. Isaac had to open the gates. Colonel Cary would write to Old Master what day he was coming. Whenever Isaac missed opening them gates in time, the Colonel soon as he git to the house, look about for him and whip him with his horse-whip. Old Master used to keep dinner for

Colonel Cary. He was a tall thin-visaged man jist like Mr. Jefferson: he drove four-in-hand. The Colonel as soon as he git out of his carriage, walk right straight into the kitchen and ax de cooks what they hab for dinner? If they didn't have what he wanted, bleeged to wait dinner till it was cooked. Colonel Cary made freer at Monticello than he did at home: whip anybody: would stay several weeks: give servants money, sometimes five or six dollars among 'em. Tuckahoe Tom Randolph married Colonel Cary's daughter Nancy. The Colonel lived at Ampthill on the James River where Colonel Bob Temple lived arterwards. Edgehill was the seat of Tom Mann Randolph, father of Jefferson Randolph: it was three miles from Monticello.

CHAPTER 13

ISAAC carred on the tin-business two years. It failed. He then carred on the nail-business at Monticello seven years: made money at that. Mr. Jefferson had the first (nail) cutting machine 'twas said, that ever was in Vaginny—sent over from England: made wrought nails and cut-nails, to shingle and lathe: sold them out of the shop: got iron rods from Philadelphia by water: boated them up from Richmond to Milton, a small town on the Rivanna: wagoned from thar.

CHAPTER 14

THOMAS Mann Randolph had ten children.[26] Isaac lived with him fust and last twenty-six or seven years: treated him mighty well: one of the finest masters in Virginia: his a wife mighty peaceable woman: never holler for servant: make no fuss nor racket: pity she ever died! Tom Mann Randolph's eldest daughter Ann, a son named Jefferson, another James, and another Benjamin. Jefferson Randolph married Mr. Nicholas'[27] daughter (Anne). Billy Giles[28] courted Miss Polly, Old Master's daughter. Isaac one morning saw him talking to her in the garden, right back of the nail-factory shop: she was lookin on de ground: all at once she wheeled round and come off.

That was the time she turned him off. Isaac never so sorry for a man in all his life: sorry because everybody thought that she was going to marry him. Mr. Giles give several dollars to the servants and when he went away dat time he never come back no more. His servant Arthur was a big man. Isaac wanted Mr. Giles to marry Miss Polly. Arthur always said that he was a mighty fine man: he was very rich: used to come to Monticello in a monstrous fine gig: mighty few gigs in dem days with plated mountins and harness.

CHAPTER 15

ELK Hill: Old Master had a small brick house there where he used to stay, about a mile from Elk Island on the North Side of the James River. The river forks there: one half runs one side of the island, tother the other side. When Mr. Jefferson was Governor, he used to stay thar a month or sich a matter and when he was at the mountain he would come and stay a month or so and then go back again. Blenheim was a low large wooden house two storeys high, eight miles from Monticello. Old Colonel Carter lived thar: had a light red head like Mr. Jefferson. Isaac know'd him and every son he had. Didn't know his daughters.

Mr. Jefferson used to hunt squirrels and partridges; kept five or six guns; oftentimes carred Isaac wid him: Old Master wouldn't shoot partridges settin: said "he wouldn't take advantage of em"—would give 'em a chance for thar life: wouldn't shoot a hare settin, nuther; skeer him up fust. "My Old Master was as neat a hand as ever you see to make keys and locks and small chains, iron and brass;" he kept all kind of blacksmith and carpenter tools in a great case with shelves to it in his library, an upstairs room. Isaac went up thar constant: been up thar a thousand times; used to car coal up thar: Old Master had a couple of small bellowses up thar.

The likeness of Mr. Jefferson (in Linn's Life of him) according to Isaac, is not much like him. "Old Master never dat handsome in dis world: dat likeness right between Old Master and Ginral Washington: Old Master was squar-shouldered." For amusement he would work sometimes in the garden for half an hour at a time in right good earnest in the cool of the evening: never know'd him to go out anywhar before breakfast.

CHAPTER 16

THE school at Monticello was in the out-chamber fifty yards off from the great house, on the same level. But the scholars went into the house to Old Master to git lessons, in the south end of the house called the South Octagon. Mrs. Skipper (Skipwith) had two daughters thar: Mrs. Eppes, one.

Mr. Jefferson's sister Polly married old Ned Bolling[29] of Chesterfield, about ten miles from Petersburg. Isaac has been thar since his death: saw the old man's grave. Mr. John Bradley owns the place now. Isaac slept in the out-chamber where the scholars was: slept on the floor in a blanket: in the winter season git up in the mornin and make fire for them. From Monticello you can see mountains all round as far as the eye can reach: sometimes see it rainin down this course and the sun shining over the tops of the clouds. Willis' Mountain sometimes looked in the cloud like a great house with two chimnies to it: fifty miles from Monticello.

CHAPTER 17

THAR was a sight of pictures at Monticello: pictures of Ginral Washington and the Marcus Lafayette. Isaac saw him fust in the old war in the mountain with Old Master; saw him agin the last time he was in Vaginny. He gave Isaac a guinea: Isaac saw him in the Capitol at Richmond and talked with him and made him sensible when he fust saw him in the old war. Thar was a large marble at Monticello with twelve angels cut on it that came from Heaven: all cut in marble.

About the time when my Old Master begun to wear spectacles, he was took with a swellin in his legs: used to bathe 'em and bandage 'em: said it was settin too much:

when he'd git up and walk it wouldn't hurt
him. Isaac and John Hemings nursed him
two months: had to car him about on a han-
barrow. John Hemings[30] went to the carpenter's trade same year Isaac went to the black-
smiths. Miss Lucy, Old Master's daughter,
died quite a small child; died down the coun-
try at Mrs. Eppes' or Mrs. Bolling's, one of
her young aunts. Old Master was embassador
to France at that time. He brought a great
many clothes from France with him: a coat
of blue cloth trimmed with gold lace; cloak
trimmed so too: dar say it weighed fifty
pounds: large buttons on the coat as big as
half a dollar; cloth set in the button: edge
shine like gold: in summer he war silk coat,
pearl buttons.

Colonel Jack Harvie[31] owned Belmont,
jinin Monticello. Four as big men as any in
Petersburg could git in his waistcoat: he
owned Belvidere, near Richmond: the Colonel died thar: monstrous big man. The
washerwoman once buttoned his waistcoat
on Isaac and three others. Mrs. Harvie was
a little woman.

CHAPTER 18

MR. JEFFERSON never had nothing to do with horse-racing or cock-fighting: bought two race-horses once, but not in their racing day: bought em arter done runnin. One was Brimmer,[32] a pretty horse with two white feet: when he bought him he was in Philadelphia: kept him thar. One day Joseph Rattiff the Frenchman was ridin him in the streets of Philadelphia: Brimmer got skeered; run agin shaft of a dray and got killed. Tother horse was Tarkill:[33] in his race-day they called him the Roane colt: only race-horse of a roane Isaac ever see: Old Master used him for a ridin-horse. Davy Watson and Billy were German soldiers:

both workmen, both smoked pipes and both drinkers: drank whiskey; git drunk and sing: take a week at a time drinkin and singin. Colonel Goode of Chesterfield was a great racer: used to visit Mr. Jefferson; had a trainer named Pompey.

Old Master had a great many rabbits: made chains for the old buck-rabbits to keep them from killin the young ones: had a rabbit-house (a warren)—a long rock house: some of em white, some blue: they used to burrow under ground. Isaac expects thar is plenty of em bout dar yit: used to eat em at Monticello. Mr. Jefferson never danced nor played cards. He had dogs named Ceres, Bull, Armandy, and Claremont: most of em French dogs: he brought em over with him from France. Bull and Ceres were bull-dogs: he brought over Buzzy with him too: she pupped at sea: Armandy and Claremont, stump-tails, both black.

CHAPTER 19

JOHN BROCK, the overseer that lived next to the great-house, had gray hounds to hunt deer. Mr. Jefferson had a large park at Monticello: built in a sort of a flat on the side of the mountain. When the hunters run the deer down thar, they'd jump into the park and couldn't git out. When Old Master heard hunters in the park he used to go down thar wid his gun and order em out. The park was two or three miles round and fenced in with a high fence, twelve rails double-staked and ridered: kept up four or five years arter Old Master was gone. Isaac and his father (George) fed the deer at sun-up and sun-down: called em up and fed em wid corn: had holes all along the fence at the feedin-place: gave em salt, got right gentle: come up and eat out of your hand.

No wild-cats at Monticello: some lower down at Buck Island: bears sometimes came on the plantation at Monticello: wolves so plenty that they had to build pens round black peoples' quarters and pen sheep in em to keep the wolves from catching them. But they killed five or six of a night in the winter season: come and steal in the pens in the night. When the snow was on the groun you could see the wolves in gangs runnin and howlin, same as a drove of hogs: made the deer run up to the feedin-place many a night. The feedin-place was right by the house whar Isaac stayed. They raised many sheep and goats at Monticello.

The woods and mountains was often on fire: Isaac has gone out to help to put out the fire: everybody would turn out from Charlottesville and everywhere: git in the woods and sometimes work all night fightin the fire.

CHAPTER 20

COLONEL CARY of Chesterfield schooled Old Master: he went to school to old Mr. Wayles. Old Master had six sisters: Polly married a Bolling; Patsy married old Dabney Carr in the lowgrounds; one married William Skipwith; Nancy married old Hastings Marks. Old Master's brother, Mass Randall,[34] was a mighty simple man: used to come out among black people, play the fiddle and dance half the night: hadn't much more sense than Isaac. Jack Eppes[35] that married Miss Polly lived at Mount Black[36] on James River and then at Edge Hill, then in Cumberland at Millbrooks. Isaac left Monticello four years before Mr. Jefferson died.[37] Tom Mann Randolph, that married Mr. Jefferson's daughter, wanted Isaac to build a threshing machine at Varina. Old Henrico Court House was thar: pulled down now. Coxendale Island (Dutch Gap) jinin Varina was an Indian Situation: when fresh come, it washed up more Indian bones than ever you see. When Isaac was a boy there want more than ten houses at Jamestown. Charlottesville then not as big as Pocahontas[38] is now. Mr. DeWitt kept tavern thar.

Isaac knowed Ginral Redhazel:[39] he stayed at Colle, Mr. Mazzei's place, two miles and a quarter from Monticello—a long wood house built by Mazzei's servants. The servants' house built of little saplins of oak and hickory instead of lathes: then plastered up: it seemed as if de folks in dem days hadn't sense enough to make lathes. The Italian people raised plenty of vegetables: cooked the most victuals of any people Isaac ever see.

Mr. Jefferson bowed to everybody he meet: talked wid his arms folded. Gave the boys in the nail-factory a pound of meat a week, a dozen herrings, a quart of molasses and peck of meal. Give them that wukked the best a suit of red or blue: encouraged them mightily. Isaac calls him a mighty good master. There would be a great many carriages at Monticello at a time, in particular when people was passing to the Springs.

Isaac is now (1847) at Petersburg, Va., seventy large odd years old: bears his years well: is a blacksmith by trade and has his shop not far from Pocahontas bridge. He is quite pleased at the idea of having his life written and protests that every word of it is true; that is, of course, according to the best of his knowledge and belief. Isaac is rather tall, of strong frame, stoops a little, in color ebony: sensible, intelligent, pleasant: wears large circular iron-bound spectacles and a leather apron. A capital daguerrotype of him was taken by a Mr. Shew. Isaac was so much pleased with it that he had one taken of his wife, a large fat round-faced good-humoured looking black woman. My attention was first drawn to Isaac by Mr. Dandridge Spotswood, who had often heard him talk about Mr. Jefferson and Monticello.

C. C.

P. S. Isaac died a few years after these his recollections were taken down. He bore a good character.

NOTES

NOTES

Except where so indicated by square brackets, the following notes are Charles Campbell's.

1. [Campbell inserts in the text the correct spelling in parentheses followed by a long note:] (Ursula*) *There was a work published in 1862 by C. Scribner, at New York, entitled: "The Private Life of Thomas Jefferson from entirely new materials with numerous facsimiles, edited by Rev. Hamilton W. Pierson, D.D., President of Cumberland College, Kentucky." This work consists of the reminiscenses of a Captain Edmund Bacon, who was overseer for Mr. Jefferson at Monticello for 20 years. The Captain's reminiscenses were taken down from his lips by Dr. Pierson. The Captain mentions Ursula among the house-servants and says: "She was Mrs. Randolph's nurse. She was a big fat woman. She took charge of all the children that were not in school. If there was any switching to be done, she always did it. She used to be down at my house a great deal with those children. They used to be there so much that we often got tired of them: but we never said so. They were all very much attached to their nurse: they always called her 'Mammy.' " Isaac in 1847, by his own estimate upwards of seventy years old, was a big fat robust black man. [For further facts about Ursula and other members of Isaac's immediate family, see the section immediately after these notes.]

2. [Campbell's compressed note on Jefferson's wife is sounder in facts than it is in syntax:] Martha, youngest daughter of John Wayles, a native of Lancaster, England, a lawyer, who lived at "the Forest" in Charles City county, Va. He was married three times and dying in May 1773 left three daughters, one of whom married Francis Eppes (Father of John W. Eppes who married Maria, daughter of Thomas Jefferson), and the other Fulwar Skipwith. Mr. Jefferson inherited the Shadwell and Monticello estates. The portion that he acquired by marriage was encumbered with a (British) debt and resulted in a heavy loss. Martha Skelton was 23 years old in 1772 when she married Mr. Jefferson. [Mrs. Jefferson was, in fact, not the youngest daughter of John Wayles, but (except for a still-born twin) the oldest. She was, however, the youngest child of Wayles' first marriage. Jefferson wrote out the details of the Wayles genealogy on a blank leaf in his Prayer Book: see the 1952 Meriden Gravure facsimile.]

3. [Campbell inserts the correct spelling:] (Bathurst)

4. Sometime Governor of Virginia.

5. [Campbell parenthetically inserts in the text the following spelling:] (Orr?)

6. Captain Bacon says: John Hemings made most of the wood-work and Joe Fosset made the iron-work.

7. [A genealogical table of the Hemings family derived from the Farm Book is given on pages 56-57.]

A Chart of the Hemings Family
Derived from Jefferson's Farm Book

(This is a continuation of footnote 7)

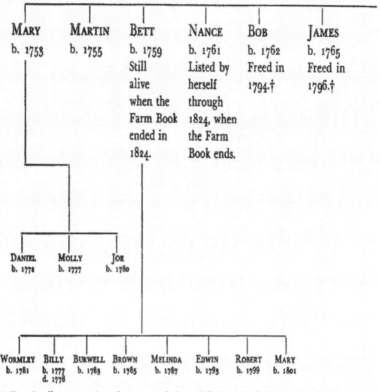

MARY	MARTIN	BETT	NANCE	BOB	JAMES
b. 1753	b. 1755	b. 1759	b. 1761	b. 1762	b. 1765
		Still	Listed by	Freed in	Freed in
		alive	herself	1794.†	1796.†
		when the	through		
		Farm Book	1824, when		
		ended in	the Farm		
		1824.	Book ends.		

DANIEL	MOLLY	JOE
b. 1772	b. 1777	b. 1780

WORMLEY	BILLY	BURWELL	BROWN	MELINDA	EDWIN	ROBERT	MARY
b. 1781	b. 1777 d. 1778	b. 1783	b. 1785	b. 1787	b. 1793	b. 1799	b. 1801

† For details concerning the manumission of Robert and James Hemings, see Edwin M. Betts' edition of *Thomas Jefferson's Farm Book*, index under Slaves. The records of these manumissions may also be found in the Order Books of the Clerk of the Albemarle County Court. The Act of the General Assembly under which Jefferson freed these slaves may be found in the Virginia Code for 1794.

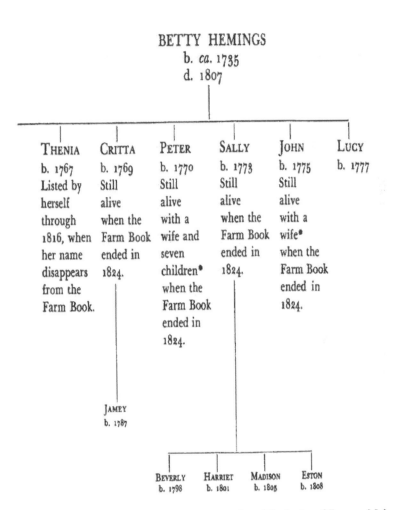

BETTY HEMINGS
b. *ca.* 1735
d. 1807

THENIA	CRITTA	PETER	SALLY	JOHN	LUCY
b. 1767	b. 1769	b. 1770	b. 1773	b. 1775	b. 1777
Listed by herself through 1816, when her name disappears from the Farm Book.	Still alive when the Farm Book ended in 1824.	Still alive with a wife and seven children* when the Farm Book ended in 1824.	Still alive when the Farm Book ended in 1824.	Still alive with a wife* when the Farm Book ended in 1824.	

JAMEY
b. 1787

BEVERLY	HARRIET	MADISON	ESTON
b. 1798	b. 1801	b. 1805	b. 1808

* The 1824 list is not subdivided by family; thus while the fact of Peter and John being alive in 1824 is readily established, the absence of information concerning the names of their wives and children makes it impossible to say for certain which other members of their families were still alive. The latest record in the Farm Book of the families of Peter and John was for the year 1810.

8. "Campbell identifies the College in a parenthetical insertion:] (of William and Mary)

9. [Campbell parenthetically defines Isaac's word "picture" as a:] (statue) [The statue of Lord Botetourt, colonial governor of Virginia from 1768 to 1770, still stands in the quadrangle of the College of William and Mary. There is a good picture of it facing page 130 in Malone's *Jefferson the Virginian*.]

10. The Rev. William Douglas, in a school at Shadwell near Monticello, instructed Young Jefferson in the rudiments of Greek, Latin and French. [Douglas was a Scottish clergyman, whose pies Jefferson remembered as being moldy and whose instruction (except in the classics) he remembered as being excellent.]

11. [Campbell parenthetically explains who Polly was:] (Maria) [i.e., Thomas Jefferson's daughter, later Mrs. John W. Eppes]

12. Robert Beverley, the historian, married Ursula Byrd of Westover, from whom the Monticello Ursula may have derived her name. [For known biographical facts concerning Isaac's mother, see the data on Isaac's family immediately following this section.]

13. [Campbell inserts the name in parentheses:] (Bathurst Skelton)

14. [Campbell parenthetically explains that the "Palace" was the:] (Governor's house). Isaac's term has adhered to the Williamsburg governors' residence, but not to the Richmond one.

15. [Campbell parenthetically indicates that the British were:] (under Arnold)

16. [Campbell supplies the date:] (Jan. 6, 1781)

17. They didn't come by way of Manchester. [For Isaac's slips in memory, or in reporting, see Logan page 5.]

18. At East end of Grace St.—now (1871) the Central Hotel.

19. [Campbell's parenthetical insertion at this point has been removed to these notes because the quotation seems clearly to have been his, not Isaac's:] (Although "All men by nature are free and equal.")

20. Captain Bacon describes him as "Six feet two and a half inches high, well proportioned and straight as a gunbarrel. He was like a fine horse: he had no surplus flesh."

21. Captain Bacon says: "He was always very neat in his dress: wore short breeches and bright shoe-buckles. When he rode on horseback he had a pair of overalls that he always put on."

22. John Walker, member of Congress during the Revolution.

23. Philip Mazzei, an Italian, author of "Recherches Sur Les Etats-Unis," 3 volumes, published at Paris in 1788.

24. Captain Bacon says: "When he was not talking he was nearly always humming some tune; or singing in a low tone to himself."

25. [Isaac is wrong here. Jefferson went to Philadelphia in 1790 as Secretary of State. See also Footnote 17.]

26. Thomas Mann Randolph's sons were Thomas Jefferson, James Madison, Benjamin Franklin, Merriwether [sic] Lewis and George Wythe (Secretary of War of C. S.) , daughters Anne, Ellen, Virginia, Cornelia and Septimia. [Thomas Mann Randolph actually had twelve children, one of whom, the first Ellen Wayles Randolph, died within a year of her birth. The children are listed in

Thomas Jefferson's Prayer Book in order of birth as fol-
lows: Anne Cary, Thomas Jefferson, Ellen Wayles, Ellen
Wayles, Cornelia, Virginia, Mary Jefferson, James, Benjamin, Lewis, Septimia, and George Wythe.]

27. Wilson Cary Nicholas, sometime Governor of Virginia.

28. [In identifying William Branch Giles, Campbell gives
the wrong middle initial:] William C. Giles, M. C., a
celebrated debater. Sometime Governor of Virginia. He
acquired the sobriquet of "Farmer Giles."

29. John Bolling, of Cobbs in Chesterfield, married a
sister [Mary] of Thomas Jefferson. [See Malone I, 38-9.]

30. Captain Bacon in his reminiscences of Mr. Jefferson
at Monticello says, "John Hemings was a carpenter. He
was a first-rate workman, a very extra workman: he could
make anything that was wanting in woodwork. He
learned his trade with Dinsmore. John Hemings made
most of the woodwork of Mr. Jefferson's fine carriage."

31. He had command of the troops of Convention for a
time.

32. According to Captain Bacon, "Brimmer was a son of
imported Knowlsby. He was a bay, but a shade darker
than any of the others. He was a horse of fair size, full,
but not quite as tall as Eagle. He was a good riding-horse
and excellent for the harness. Mr. Jefferson broke all his
horses to both ride and work. I bought Brimmer of
General John H. Cocke of Fluvanna County." [Bacon's
"Brimmer" is, of course, a corruption of "Bremo." See
Betts, *Thomas Jefferson's Farm Book*, index under
Horses.]

33. [Campbell inserts the correct spelling in the text:]
(Tarquin?) [Jefferson purchased Tarquin in 1790 from

William Fitzhugh and gave him to Thomas Mann Randolph in 1793. See Betts, *Thomas Jefferson's Farm Book*, page 96.]

34. [Campbell inserts the correct spelling:] (Randolph) [For details of Randolph Jefferson, see Mayo, *Thomas Jefferson and His Unknown Brother.*]

35. [Campbell inserts the full name:] (John W. Eppes, M. C.)

36. [Campbell guesses that this was:] (Mt. Blanc?)

37. [Isaac is wrong here. The Farm Book indicates that Isaac was living at Monticello until at least 1824, when the book ended, which was only two years before Jefferson's death. See also footnote 17.]

38. [Campbell describes Pocahontas as:] (a village on the Appomattox, opposite Petersburg)

39. [Campbell gives the correct spelling in parentheses:] (Riedesel, commander of the German troops of Convention.)

BIOGRAPHICAL DATA CONCERNING ISAAC

Aside from Isaac's own reminiscences, the chief sources of information about him are in the writings, published and unpublished, of Thomas Jefferson. Chief of these is the Farm Book (a register of slaves: their births, deaths, food and clothing issues, their location on the plantations, etc.) kept by Jefferson sporadically from 1774 to 1824. There is a break in the Farm Book from 1801 to 1810, during and just after Jefferson's two terms as President. Notes about Isaac are also in the Book of Nail Manufacturing, and there are occasional mentions of him in the Account Books.

The following data concerning Isaac all derive from the Jefferson manuscripts and are entirely independent of either Charles Campbell or Isaac's own reminiscences.

Isaac was born at Monticello in December, 1775, although his birth date is twice incorrectly listed by Jefferson in later years as 1768. He was the son of Great George, who was born in 1730, was living at Monticello in 1774 when the Farm Book begins, and died at Monticello in 1799. Great George's wife, Isaac's mother, was Ursula, who was born in 1738 and was bought by Jefferson from Fleming's estate on January 21, 1773. She died at Monticello in 1800. Isaac had three brothers: Little George and Bagwell, who came to Monticello in 1773 with Ursula when they were 14 and 5 years old respectively; and Archy, born at Monticello in 1773, who died before Isaac's birth.

Isaac lived at Monticello during most of the years between 1775 and 1824. Although he says in his memoirs that he left Monticello four years before Jefferson died, it is clear from the Farm Book that he lived there at least until two years before Jefferson's death, when the Farm Book ends. Isaac first appears in the Farm Book at the time of his birth; his first listing as a smith is on Jefferson's slave roll in 1794, and some of the accounts of his products in the nail factory are available for 1796. In 1796 and 1797 he was living with Iris, a slave born at Monticello in the same year as Isaac. His name appears with hers and those of her two sons (Squire, born in 1793, and Joyce, "a boy" born in 1796), so bracketed as to indicate that the children may both have been his. The names of Iris and her children disappear from the Farm Book in 1798, and Isaac then remained single until 1816, when his name was linked for two years with that of Suckey. Suckey was not an uncommon name among the Monticello slaves: there are seven listed in the Farm Book with specific birth dates between the years 1765 and 1806, and several more without birth dates. Of these, two at least were still alive in 1824, and scraps of additional information about each of them can be pieced together. Which Suckey was connected with Isaac, and what happened to the relationship in 1818, when one of the Suckeys was leased to Thomas Jefferson Randolph, remains in doubt. There is a reasonable probability that Isaac's "large fat round-faced good-humored looking black woman" of the 1840's was not one of these Suckeys, but a successor.

At some time during Isaac's life at Monticello, he became the property of Jefferson's son-in-law, Thomas Mann Randolph. Jefferson wrote to Randolph on January 25, 1798, "You will of course take Isaac when you please," and Jefferson's Account Book for 1812 has these three equivocal entries concerning Isaac:

Jan. 30. pd Samuel Grosse jailer of Bath county for TMRandolph 30. D[ollars]. for taking up & bringing Isaac home. on account.

Nov. 8 gave TMR's Isaac on finish[in]g the chimney of the Factory 1. D[ollar]. h[ouse]h[ol]d exp[enses] 1. D[ollar].

Dec. 21. Isaac for a truss for Abram. 1. D[ollar].
h[ouse]h[ol]d exp[enses] 2.125 [Dollars].*

The following genealogical table of Isaac's immediate family is derived from the Farm Book.

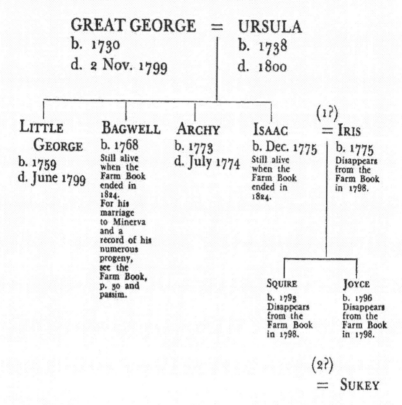

* The dollar mark ($) had already come into use in
some of the eastern states, but Jefferson was never to use
this new-fangled annotation, at least in his account books.
It will be noted that this 1812 entry was early enough for
the so-called "bit" or 12 ½-cent piece to have a meaning.
It survives today only in pairs as the quarter-dollar, or
"two-bit" piece.

66

BIOGRAPHICAL DATA CONCERNING CHARLES CAMPBELL

Charles Campbell was born in Petersburg, Virginia, on May 1, 1807. After graduating from the College of New Jersey with a law degree, he began a career as a school teacher. In 1842 he started his own school in Petersburg, and from 1855 to 1870 served as principal of Anderson Seminary.

Campbell was both an author and a collector of historical writings. Much of his collected manuscript material was lent to Bishop William Meade of Virginia, who used it in his two volumes on *Old Churches and Families of Virginia*. As an author, Campbell contributed regularly to *The Southern Literary Messenger* and to the *Virginia Historical Register*. His *Introduction to the History of the Colony and Ancient Dominion of Virginia* was published in Richmond in 1847, the date Campbell gives in the *Memoirs* for his interview with Isaac, and was republished in an enlarged edition at Philadelphia in 1860. Campbell was the author also of a *Genealogy of the Spotswood Family* and editor of the *Bland Papers* and *Some Materials to Serve for a Brief Memoir of*

John Daly Burk, Author of a History of Virginia.

Campbell died in the Staunton Lunatic Asylum on July 11, 1876, after some years of invalidism. The Isaac Jefferson manuscript, however, was prepared for publication in 1871, several years before Campbell's breakdown, and the manuscript itself indicates that Campbell was in full possession of his mental powers at the time that he wrote it.

Further information concerning Charles Campbell may be found in Rayford Logan's introduction to the 1951 edition of Isaac's *Memoirs* and through the list of published biographical notices appended to Edward A. Wyatt's own sketch of Campbell in *Virginia Imprint Series, No. 9: Preliminary Checklist for Petersburg,* Richmond, 1949, p.274-5.

NOTE ON THE ILLUSTRATIONS

ISAAC JEFFERSON

The frontispiece is from a photograph of a daguerreotype, showing Isaac probably at the time he was working in Petersburg in the 1840's. For Campbell's comments on it, see page 52. Taken by a Mr. Shew, probably in Petersburg, it was one of a pair: the daguerreotype of Isaac's wife made at the same time has apparently not survived. The picture is probably the earliest existing photographic likeness of a slave. John T. Winterich in commenting on it said (in the *Saturday Review*, February 23, 1952, p. 13) "It gives one something of a shock to inspect a photograph of a man who accompanied our first Secretary of State to Philadelphia in 1790."

The daguerreotype is now in the Tracy W. McGregor Library at the University of Virginia.

JEFFERSON'S LIFE MASK

The plaster life mask of Jefferson was made by John H. I. Browere at Monticello in 1825, the year before Jefferson's death, and presumably within a twelvemonth of Isaac's departure. Jefferson described the ordeal of the mask making in a letter to James Madison, October 18, 1825: "Successive coats of thin grout plaistered on the naked head, and kept there an hour, would have been a severe trial of a young and hale person. He [Browere] suffered the plaister also to get so dry that separation became difficult & even dangerous. He was obliged to use freely the mallet & chisel to break it into pieces and get off a piece at a time. These thumps of the mallet would have been sensible almost to a loggerhead. The family became alarmed, and he confused, till I was quite exhausted, and there became real danger that the ears would separate from the head sooner than from the plaister. I now bid adieu for ever to busts & even portraits." For a view of the mask from another angle, see F. C. Rosenberger's *Jefferson Reader*, facing page 257.

The life mask is now at the New York State Historical Association, and is reproduced here through the courtesy of Miss Mary E. Cunningham and the Association.

JEFFERSON'S POLYGRAPH

Jefferson's polygraph was presented to the University of Virginia in 1875 by Jefferson's grandson and is now on permanent loan to Monticello. The following letter accompanied Mr. Randolph's gift:

June 30th 1875
Edge Hill

The Honorable Board of Visitors of the University of Va.

Gentlemen

Allow me through your body to present to the University the polygraph used [by] Mr. Jefferson for the last twenty years of his life. In retrieving [?] for publication many thousand of these letters, they [the polygraph copies] were found accurate facsimilies of his handwriting; no error [occurring] except where the record pen was caught by some irregularity in the paper. When extricating itself with a spring, it missed a few letters, leaving space for them.

Most respectfully
Thos. J. Randolph, Sr.

P.S. Copies from this polygraph remain perfect and unfaded when those made by the copying press are illegible.

The photograph was made by Ralph Thompson.

LINN ENGRAVING OF JEFFERSON

William Linn's *Life of Thomas Jefferson* was first published in 1834 and was republished in 1839 and 1843. The frontispiece shown to Isaac by Campbell appeared in all three editions. It was engraved by Stephen H. Gimber from the Stuart portrait of Jefferson of 1823, which was in turn copied by Stuart from his earlier (ca. 1805) life portrait of Jefferson, showing the President in his early sixties. Gimber's engraving was, thus, a poor reproduction of a not too successful copy of a life portrait, representing Jefferson about twenty years younger than Isaac would have remembered him.

For further details of the likenesses of Jefferson, see Fiske Kimball's *The Life Portraits of Jefferson and Their Replicas*, Philadelphia, 1944.

MONTICELLO

This 1826 watercolor of Monticello, probably drawn by some immediate member of Jefferson's family, shows the southwest front of the house and gardens at about the time Isaac left there. It survived as part of the Jefferson-Coolidge Papers and was reproduced in black and white through the courtesy of Mrs. T. Jefferson Coolidge by Francis Calley Gray in his *Thomas Jefferson in 1814* (Boston, 1924, between p. 20-21) and by Fiske Kimball in his *Jefferson's Grounds and Gardens at Monticello* (New York, 1926? p. 15). The first reproduction of the drawing in color (through the courtesy of George H. Cushing, Jr.) was in the *Virginia Cavalcade* (Vol. 1, Spring 1952, p. 4), published by the Virginia State Library. It is through the kindness of Mr. Randolph W. Church, Librarian of the Virginia State Library, that the color plates for this earliest known picture of Monticello are used here.

BIBLIOGRAPHICAL NOTE

The manuscript from which the text of the *Memoirs* is printed is in the Tracy W. McGregor Library at the University of Virginia. Campbell entitled it "Life of Isaac Jefferson of Petersburg, Virginia, Blacksmith, containing a full and faithful account of Monticello and the Family there, with notices of many of the distinguished characters that visited there, with his Revolutionary experience and travels, adventures, observations and opinions, the whole taken down from his own words." For detailed notes on its provenance and for a comparison with a similar manuscript at William and Mary, see the scholarly edition of 1951 edited by Rayford W. Logan. In transcribing this same manuscript, Dr. Logan aimed at absolute literalness, preserving all spelling, capitalization, and punctuation exactly as it appeared in Campbell's manuscript. In the present edition, an attempt has been made to normalize the transcription, changing Campbell's punctuation, capitalization, and spelling where necessary to make the narrative read more easily. Care was, however, taken to retain any original spelling that seemed to reflect Isaac's pronunciation. Some of Campbell's parenthetical insertions and all of his footnotes have been placed at the end of Isaac's narrative. There are no omissions or suppressions from the text, and information derived from other sources is clearly indicated as such.

The chief published primary documents are to be found in the *Papers of Thomas Jefferson,* edited by Julian P. Boyd (1950-   ), and in *Thomas Jefferson's Farm Book,* edited by Edwin M. Betts (1954). The chief unpublished primary sources (e.g., the Account Books and the Book of Nail Manufacturing) may all be consulted in photostat at the University of Virginia.

Readers interested in the background of Isaac Jefferson's life are referred especially to the Betts edition of *Thomas Jefferson's Farm Book* (Princeton), to Bernard Mayo's *Jefferson Himself,* to Francis C. Rosenberger's anthology, *The Jefferson Reader* (Dutton), and to two older biographies of Thomas Jefferson: Sarah Randolph's *Domestic Life* (1871) and Henry S. Randall's *Life* (1858). The current standard biographies of Jefferson are: Dumas Malone's (Little, B r o w n), Gilbert Chinard's (Little, Brown), and Marie Kimball's (Coward-McCann).

INDEX

INDEX